Printable PDF forms – KG Meyer, P.C.
For Year 20____

The following pages contain the full-size worksheets in printable 8.5" x 11" PDF.

Notes and Comments:

ONLINE INFORMATION RECORD

Website Name or Address	User Name/ID	Password	PIN/Other #

ACCOUNT INFORMATION

Account Number	Password Hint/Q&A	Tech Support Number	Notes

Net Worth

Date Completed _____

ASSETS–WHAT YOU OWN

	Amount
Cash: On Hand	_____
Checking Accounts	_____
Savings Accounts	_____
Money Markets	_____
Other	_____

Real Estate/Property (current market value):

	Amount
Principal Residence	_____
Second Residence	_____
Land	_____
Income Property	_____
Other (business, partnerships, etc.)	_____

Investments (market value):

	Amount
Cash Value Life Insurance	_____
Certificates of Deposit	_____
U.S. Treasury Bills/Savings Bonds	_____
Stocks	_____
Bonds	_____
Mutual Funds	_____
College Fund (529 Plans, etc.)	_____
Limited Partnerships	_____
Annuities	_____
IRA—Regular/Roth	_____
Keogh/SEP Plans	_____
401(k), 403(b), or 457 Plans	_____
Pension Plan/Retirement Plans	_____
Other (stock options, bonuses, etc.)	_____

Personal Loans Receivable _____

Personal Property (current market value):

	Amount
Cars, Trucks, Vehicles	_____
Recreational Vehicle/Watercraft	_____
Electronic Equipment	_____
Home Furnishings	_____
Home Entertainment	_____
Equipment/Tools	_____
Appliances and Furniture	_____
Collectibles/Antiques	_____
Jewelry and Furs Other:	_____

Total Assets $ _____

LIABILITIES–WHAT YOU OWE

	Amount

Current Debts:

	Amount
Household	_____
Medical	_____
Credit Card 1 Credit Card 2 Credit Card 3	_____
Department Store Cards	_____
Back Taxes (Federal, State, Property)	_____
Legal	_____
Child Support	_____
Alimony Other:	_____
Other:	_____

Mortgages:

	Amount
Principal Residence	_____
Second Residence	_____
Land	_____
Income Property Other:	_____
Other:	_____

Loans:

	Amount
Home Equity (HELOC)	_____
Bank/Finance Company	_____
Automobiles, Vehicles	_____
Recreational Vehicle/Watercraft	_____
Education/Student	_____
Life Insurance	_____
Personal (from family or friends)	_____
Retirement Accounts	_____
Thrift Savings Plan Other:	_____

Total Liabilities $ _____

Total Assets $ _____ − Total Liabilities $ _____ = Net Worth $ _____

IDENTIFIED GOALS WORKSHEET

INTERMEDIATE/SHORT RANGE GOALS

Priority	Goal	Target Date	Cost Estimate	Amount Already Saved	How to Achieve (amount per month, second job, ect)

MIDDLE AND LONG RANGE GOALS

Priority	Goal	Target Date	Cost Estimate	Amount Already Saved	How to Achieve (amount per month, second job, ect)

GOALS SAVINGS RECORD

Goal: Roth IRA
Total Cost: 3,500

	JAN.	FEB.	MAR.	APR.	MAY	JUNE	JULY	AUG.	SEPT.	OCT.	NOV.	DEC.	
Deposit	292	292	250	275	350	292	270	320	292	292	290	285	Monthly Avg. Deposit: 292
Balance	292	584	834	1,109	1,459	1,751	2,021	2,341	2,633	2,925	3,215	3,500	**Total:** 3,500

Goal:
Total Cost:

	JAN.	FEB.	MAR.	APR.	MAY	JUNE	JULY	AUG.	SEPT.	OCT.	NOV.	DEC.	
Deposit													Monthly Avg. Deposit:
Balance													**Total:**

Goal:
Total Cost:

	JAN.	FEB.	MAR.	APR.	MAY	JUNE	JULY	AUG.	SEPT.	OCT.	NOV.	DEC.	
Deposit													Monthly Avg. Deposit:
Balance													**Total:**

Goal:
Total Cost:

	JAN.	FEB.	MAR.	APR.	MAY	JUNE	JULY	AUG.	SEPT.	OCT.	NOV.	DEC.	
Deposit													Monthly Avg. Deposit:
Balance													**Total:**

Goal:
Total Cost:

	JAN.	FEB.	MAR.	APR.	MAY	JUNE	JULY	AUG.	SEPT.	OCT.	NOV.	DEC.	
Deposit													Monthly Avg. Deposit:
Balance													**Total:**

Goal:
Total Cost:

	JAN.	FEB.	MAR.	APR.	MAY	JUNE	JULY	AUG.	SEPT.	OCT.	NOV.	DEC.	
Deposit													Monthly Avg. Deposit:
Balance													**Total:**

GOALS SAVING RECORDS CONT.

Goal:
Total Cost:

	JAN.	FEB.	MAR.	APR.	MAY	JUNE	JULY	AUG.	SEPT.	OCT.	NOV.	DEC.	
Deposit													Monthly Avg. Deposit:
Balance													**Total:**

Goal:
Total Cost:

	JAN.	FEB.	MAR.	APR.	MAY	JUNE	JULY	AUG.	SEPT.	OCT.	NOV.	DEC.	
Deposit													Monthly Avg. Deposit:
Balance													**Total:**

Goal:
Total Cost:

	JAN.	FEB.	MAR.	APR.	MAY	JUNE	JULY	AUG.	SEPT.	OCT.	NOV.	DEC.	
Deposit													Monthly Avg. Deposit:
Balance													**Total:**

The formula for determining the monthly amount to save for each of your goals is:

Total cost of your goal ÷ Number of months left to date needed = Amount per month you need to save.

NEEDS/WANTS LIST
PARENTS

Date	Item	Need	Want	Source (store, Internet, catalog, other)	Cost

CHILDREN

Date	Item	Need	Want	Source (store, Internet, catalog, other)	Cost

SUGGESTION LIST—ADDITIONAL NON-MONTHLY EXPENSES

You can either complete this information here and then transfer it to the Yearly Budget Worksheet or use this as your guideline as you fill in the worksheet directly from these ideas.

Some of the expenses listed may be a monthly expense for you. If so, enter those expenses on the Monthly Budget Worksheet, not here. The focus of the Yearly Budget Worksheet is only on the periodic, quarterly, semi-annual, annual, and non-monthly expenses to help you remember and anticipate them ahead of time.

	DESCRIPTION	AMOUNT(S)	MONTH(S) DUE
Housing	Property Taxes		
	Homeowner's/Renter's Insurance		
	Association Dues		
	Storage/PO Box		
	Yard/Equipment Repairs		
	Yard Service		
	Pool Maintenance		
	Pest Control		
	Security System		
	Home Improvement		
	Home Repairs		
	Carpet/Window Cleaning		
	Dry Cleaning Household		
	Home Decorating		
	Furniture/Appliances		
	Maintenance Agreements		
	Other		
Utilities (Non Monthly)	Fuel/Propane		
	Firewood		
	Waste Management		
	Water Softner		
	Other		
Trans	Vehicle #1 Insurance		
	Vehicle #2 Insurance		
	Boat/Recreational Vehicle		
	Emission Inspection		
	License Renewal		
	Oil Change/Tune Up		
	Maintenance/Repairs		
	Other		
Health	Insurance		
	Medical Exams/Labs		
	Visits		
	Physicals		
	Prescriptions		
	Misc Visits		
	Dental		
	Vision		
	Alternative Health		
	Vitamins/Supplements		
	Other		

SUGGESTION LIST—ADDITIONAL NON-MONTHLY EXPENSES

	DESCRIPTION	AMOUNT(S)	MONTH(S) DUE
Insurance (Oter)	Life		
	Umbrella		
	Disability		
	Long-Term Care		
	Other		
Memberships	Church/Temple		
	Country Club		
	Credit Card Fees		
	Gym		
	Organizations/Clubs		
	Professional Dues		
	Auto Club		
	Warehouse Clubs		
	Other		
Computer	Hardware/Software		
	Upgrades		
	Service/Maintenance		
	Classes/Training		
Education Adults	Tuition		
	Books/Supplies		
	Magazines/Newspapers		
	Workshops		
	Other		
Clothing	Work/Uniforms		
	Seasonal/Shoes		
	Sports/Special Events		
	Dry Cleaning		
Recreation	Parties		
	Concerts/Sporting Events		
	Fees		
	Hobbies		
	Boat/Plane Storage		
	Other		
Vacation	Transportation		
	Lodging/Meals		
	Activities		
	Shopping/Souvenris		
Children	Tuition		
	School Supplies		
	Photo/Yearbook		
	Prom/Dances		
	Field Trips/Fund Raising		
	Camps		
	Sports		
	Music Lessons		
	Care		
	Other		

SUGGESTION LIST—ADDITIONAL NON-MONTHLY EXPENSES

	DESCRIPTION	AMOUNT(S)	MONTH(S) DUE
Pets	Food		
	Toys		
	Grooming		
	Day Care/Sitter		
	Vet/Shots		
	Training		
Misc	Donations		
	Tax Preparation		
	Taxes Due/Estimated Taxes		
	Retirement		

YEARLY MONTHLY WORKSHEET   YEAR 20_____

		JAN.	FEB.	MAR.	APR.	MAY	JUNE	JULY	AUG.	SEPT.	OCT.	NOV.	DEC.	TOTAL	MO. AVG.
Housing	Property Tax														
	Homeowners Insurance														
	Home/Yard Maintenance														
	Utilities														
Transportation	Auto Insurance														
	Auto Expenses														
Health	Insurance—Other														
	Medical Expenses														
	Dental/Vision Expenses														
Additional Non-Monthly Expenses	Dues/Fees														
	Education/Tuition														
	Clothing														
	Recreation														
	Vacation/Trips														
	Gifts—Birthday														
	Gifts—Other														
	Holiday Events														
	Children's Activities														
	Pets														
	Total														

Reserve Savings: Total Expenses $ _____ divided by 12 = $ _____ /Month

GIFT GIVING WORKSHEET

	Name	Amount: Christmas/ Hanukkah	Amount: Birthday	Actual Month Due	Other Events Happening*	Amount: Other Events	Actual Month Due
Spouse		$	$			$	
Parents/Self							
Children/Grandchildren							
Sisters/Brothers							
Grandparents							

* Other: Anniversaries, weddings, showers, babies, Mother's Day, Father's Day, graduations, Bar/Bat Mitzvahs, religious events

GIFT GIVING WORKSHEET CONT.

	Name	Amount: Christmas/ Hanukkah	Amount: Birthday	Actual Month Due	Other Events Happening*	Amount: Other Events	Actual Month Due
Aunts/Uncles		$	$			$	
Nieces/Nephews							
Friends/Work/Other							
Children's Friends							
	Total of both pages	$	$			$	

* Other: Anniversaries, weddings, showers, babies, Mother's Day, Father's Day, graduations, Bar/Bat Mitzvahs, religious events

CHRISTMAS HOLDIAY EXPENSE WORKSHEET

Item	Estimate	Already Have	Actual Cost
Tree/Wreath			
Lights—House/Tree			
Baked Goods/Gingerbread House			
Parties/Food/Liquor/Beverages/Host Gifts			
Poinsettias/Candles/Decorations/Crafts			
Gift Wrap/Greeting Cards			
Postage/Shipping/Boxes			
Digital Photo Processing/Family Portraits			
Clothes/Shoes/Jewelry			
Meals Out			
Movies/Ballet/Plays/Galleries/Travel/Tour			
Workplace Events			
Donations			
Batteries/Misc. (for gifts) Other			
Total Amount			

SOURCE OF MONEY FOR GIFTS AND HOLIDAY EXPENSES

                                                                                                  Amount Needed

Total Amount for Gifts:

(See Gift Giving Worksheet) $ _____

Total Amount—Holiday Expenses:
(See worksheet above) $ _____

TOTAL AMOUNT NEEDED for Gifts and Holiday Expenses: $ _____

List how much is available from the following sources to cover these holiday expenses:

Total Amount Available		
Source	Amount	Notes
Current Income		
Overtime/Part-Time Job		
Savings Account(s)		
Gift Money/Bonus		
Total Amount Available to Cover Expenses		
Total Amount Needed for Gifts & Holiday Expenses		
Amount Short/Extra*		

* Total amount needed – Total amount available to cover expenses = Amount short or extra Outline a plan for covering amount that is short for holiday expenses:

Source	Amount	Notes
Overtime/Part-Time Job		
Charge on Credit Cards		
Borrow		
Other		
Total Amount Need to Borrow		

MONTHLY BUDGET WORKSHEET   JANUARY

					Checking Bal.				Reserve Savings
	① Net Income Total Amount								
	Expenses	① Amount	Date Due	Paid	Date ② Rcv.:				
Fixed Amounts	Mortgage/Rent								
	Car Payments								
	Other Loans:								
	Internet Access								
	Day Care								
	Insurance								
	Insurance								
	Clubs/Dues								
	Savings—Emergency								
	Savings—Goals								
	Savings—Reserve								
	Allowance								
Fixed Variable	Electricity								
	Heating Oil/Gas								
	Water								
	Garbage								
	Telephone/Cell Phone								
	Cable TV								
	Groceries								
	Meals Out								
	Auto/Gas								
	Auto								
	Child Allowance								
	Charity								
Occasional	Household Supplies								
	Personal								
	Clothes								
	Medical								
	School Exp.								
	Recreation								
	Counseling								
	Media (Books)								
Installment	Credit Cards:								
	Visa								
	MC								
Total	Total Income								
	Total Exp. Excludes								
	Total Excess								
	Total Short								

MONTHLY BUDGET WORKSHEET FEBRUARY

	INCOME SOURCE			Checking Bal.				Reserve Savings
	① Net Income Total Amount							
	Expenses	① Amount	Date Due	Date Paid	Date ② Rcv.:			
Fixed Amounts	Mortgage/Rent							
	Car Payments							
	Other Loans:							
	Internet Access							
	Day Care							
	Insurance							
	Insurance							
	Clubs/Dues							
	Savings — Emergency							
	Savings — Goals							
	Savings — Reserve							
	Allowance							
Fixed Variable	Electricity							
	Heating Oil/Gas							
	Water							
	Garbage							
	Telephone/Cell Phone							
	Cable TV							
	Groceries							
	Meals Out							
	Auto/Gas							
	Auto							
	Child Allowance							
	Charity							
Occasional	Household Supplies							
	Personal							
	Clothes							
	Medical							
	School Exp.							
	Recreation							
	Counseling							
	Meds (Bontril)							
Installment	Credit Cards:							
	Visa							
	MC							
Total	Total Income							
	Total Exp. Excludes							
	Total Excess							
	Total Short							

MONTHLY BUDGET WORKSHEET   MARCH

					Checking Bal.				Reserve Savings
	① Net Income Total Amount								
	Expenses	① Amount	Date Due	Date Paid	Date ② Rcv.:				
Fixed Amounts	Mortgage/Rent								
	Car Payments								
	Other Loans:								
	Internet Access								
	Day Care								
	Insurance								
	Insurance								
	Clubs/Dues								
	Savings – Emergency								
	Savings – Goals								
	Savings – Reserve								
	Allowance								
Fixed Variable	Electricity								
	Heating Oil/Gas								
	Water								
	Garbage								
	Telephone/Cell Phone								
	Cable TV								
	Groceries								
	Meals Out								
	Auto/Gas								
	Auto								
	Child Allowance								
	Charity								
Occasional	Household Supplies								
	Personal								
	Clothes								
	Medical								
	School Exp.								
	Recreation								
	Counseling								
	Meals (Dates)								
Installment	Credit Cards:								
	Visa								
	MC								
Total ③	Total Income								
	Total Exp. Excludes								
	Total Excess								
	Total Short								

MONTHLY BUDGET WORKSHEET APRIL

					Checking Bal.				Reserve Savings
	① Net Income Total Amount								
		Expenses	② Amount	Date Due	Date Paid	Date ② Rcv.:			
Fixed Amounts		Mortgage/Rent							
		Car Payments							
		Other Loans:							
		Internet Access							
		Day Care							
		Insurance							
		Insurance							
		Clubs/Dues							
		Savings — Emergency							
		Savings — Goals							
		Savings — Reserve							
		Allowance							
Fixed Variable		Electricity							
		Heating Oil/Gas							
		Water							
		Garbage							
		Telephone/Cell Phone							
		Cable TV							
		Groceries							
		Meals Out							
		Auto/Gas							
		Auto							
		Child Allowance							
		Charity							
Occasional		Household Supplies							
		Personal							
		Clothes							
		Medical							
		School Exp.							
		Recreation							
		Counseling							
		Media (Books)							
Installment		Credit Cards:							
		Visa							
		MC							
Total		Total Income							
	③	Total Exp. Excludes							
		Total Excess							
		Total Short							

MONTHLY BUDGET WORKSHEET   MAY

					Checking Bal.				Reserve Savings
	① Net Income Total Amount								
	Expenses	② Amount	Date Due	Date Paid	Date ② Rcv.:				
Fixed Amounts	Mortgage/Rent								
	Car Payments								
	Other Loans:								
	Internet Access								
	Day Care								
	Insurance								
	Insurance								
	Clubs/Dues								
	Savings — Emergency								
	Savings — Goals								
	Savings — Reserve								
	Allowance								
Fixed Variable	Electricity								
	Heating Oil/Gas								
	Water								
	Garbage								
	Telephone/Cell Phone								
	Cable TV								
	Groceries								
	Meals Out								
	Auto/Gas								
	Auto								
	Child Allowance								
	Charity								
Occasional	Household Supplies								
	Personal								
	Clothes								
	Medical								
	School Exp.								
	Recreation								
	Counseling								
	Meals (Dates)								
Installment	Credit Cards:								
	Visa								
	MC								
Total ③	Total Income								
	Total Exp. Excludes								
	Total Excess								
	Total Short								

MONTHLY BUDGET WORKSHEET   JUNE

					Checking Bal.				Reserve Savings
	① Net Income Total Amount								
	Expenses	① Amount	Date Due	Date Paid	Date ② Rcv.:				
Fixed Amounts	Mortgage/Rent								
	Car Payments								
	Other Loans:								
	Internet Access								
	Day Care								
	Insurance								
	Insurance								
	Clubs/Dues								
	Savings – Emergency								
	Savings – Goals								
	Savings – Reserve								
	Allowance								
Fixed Variable	Electricity								
	Heating Oil/Gas								
	Water								
	Garbage								
	Telephone/Cell Phone								
	Cable TV								
	Groceries								
	Meals Out								
	Auto/Gas								
	Auto								
	Child Allowance								
	Charity								
Occasional	Household Supplies								
	Personal								
	Clothes								
	Medical								
	School Exp.								
	Recreation								
	Counseling								
	Mail in (Rents)								
Installment	Credit Cards:								
	Visa								
	MC								
Total	Total Income								
	Total Exp. Excludes								
	Total Excess								
	Total Short								

MONTHLY BUDGET WORKSHEET   JULY

					Checking Bal.				Reserve Savings
	① Net Income Total Amount								
	Expenses	③ Amount	Date Due	Date Paid	Date ② Rcv.:				
Fixed Amounts ④	Mortgage/Rent								
	Car Payments								
	Other Loans:								
	Internet Access								
	Day Care								
	Insurance								
	Insurance								
	Clubs/Dues								
	Savings — Emergency								
	Savings — Goals								
	Savings — Reserve								
	Allowance								
Fixed Variable	Electricity								
	Heating Oil/Gas								
	Water								
	Backups								
	Telephone/Cell Phone								
	Cable TV								
	Groceries								
	Meals Out								
	Auto/Gas								
	Auto								
	Child Allowances								
	Charity								
Occasional	Household Supplies								
	Personal								
	Clothes								
	Medical								
	School Exp.								
	Recreation								
	Counseling								
	Meals (Books)								
Installment	Credit Cards:								
	Visa								
	MC								
Total ⑤	Total Income								
	Total Exp. Excludes								
	Total Excess								
	Total Short								

MONTHLY BUDGET WORKSHEET   AUGUST

	INCOME SOURCE				Checking Bal.				Reserve Savings
	① Net Income Total Amount								
	Expenses	① Amount	Date Due	Date Paid	Date ② Rcv.:				
Fixed Amounts ④	Mortgage/Rent								
	Car Payments								
	Other Loans:								
	Internet Access								
	Day Care								
	Insurance								
	Insurance								
	Clubs/Dues								
	Savings — Emergency								
	Savings — Goals								
	Savings — Reserve								
	Allowance								
Fixed Variable	Electricity								
	Heating Oil/Gas								
	Water								
	Sludge								
	Telephone/Cell Phone								
	Cable TV								
	Groceries								
	Meals Out								
	Auto/Gas								
	Auto								
	Child Allowance								
	Charity								
Occasional	Household Supplies								
	Personal								
	Clothes								
	Medical								
	School Exp.								
	Recreation								
	Counseling								
	Meal in (Dents)								
Installment	Credit Cards:								
	Visa								
	MC								
Total ⑤	Total Income								
	Total Exp. Excludes								
	Total Excess								
	Total Short								

MONTHLY BUDGET WORKSHEET　　　　　　　　　　　　　　　SEPTEMBER

					Checking Bal.					Reserve Savings
	① Net Income Total Amount									
	Expenses	② Amount	Date Due	Date Paid	Date ② Rcv.:					
Fixed Amounts	Mortgage/Rent									
	Car Payments									
	Other Loans:									
	Internet Access									
	Day Care									
	Insurance									
	Insurance									
	Clubs/Dues									
	Savings — Emergency									
	Savings — Goals									
	Savings — Reserve									
	Allowance									
Fixed Variable	Electricity									
	Heating Oil/Gas									
	Water									
	Garbage									
	Telephone/Cell Phone									
	Cable TV									
	Groceries									
	Meals Out									
	Auto/Gas									
	Auto									
	Child Allowance									
	Charity									
Occasional	Household Supplies									
	Personal									
	Clothes									
	Medical									
	School Exp.									
	Recreation									
	Counseling									
	Media (Books)									
Installment	Credit Cards:									
	Visa									
	MC									
Total ③	Total Income									
	Total Exp. Excludes									
	Total Excess									
	Total Short									

MONTHLY BUDGET WORKSHEET   OCTOBER

	INCOME SOURCE			Checking Bal.				Reserve Savings
	① Net Income Total Amount							
	Expenses	③ Amount	Date Due	Date Paid	Date ② Rcv.:			
Fixed Amounts	Mortgage/Rent							
	Car Payments							
	Other Loans							
	Internet Access							
	Day Care							
	Insurance							
	Insurance							
	Clubs/Dues							
	Savings — Emergency							
	Savings — Goals							
	Savings — Reserve							
	Allowance							
Fixed Variable	Electricity							
	Heating Oil/Gas							
	Water							
	Garbage							
	Telephone/Cell Phone							
	Cable TV							
	Groceries							
	Meals Out							
	Auto/Gas							
	Auto							
	Child Allowance							
	Charity							
Occasional	Household Supplies							
	Personal							
	Clothes							
	Medical							
	School Exp.							
	Recreation							
	Counseling							
	Meals (Dates)							
Installment	Credit Cards							
	Visa							
	MC							
Total	Total Income							
	Total Exp. Excludes							
	Total Excess							
	Total Short							

MONTHLY BUDGET WORKSHEET NOVEMBER

			Date		Checking Bal. Date ②				Reserve Savings
	① Net Income Total Amount								
	Expenses	① Amount	Due	Paid	Rcv.:				
Fixed Amounts	Mortgage/Rent								
	Car Payments								
	Other Loans:								
	Internet Access								
	Day Care								
	Insurance								
	Insurance								
	Clubs/Dues								
	Savings – Emergency								
	Savings – Goals								
	Savings – Reserve								
	Allowance								
Fixed Variable	Electricity								
	Heating Oil/Gas								
	Water								
	Garbage								
	Telephone/Cell Phone								
	Cable TV								
	Groceries								
	Meals Out								
	Auto/Gas								
	Auto								
	Child Allowances								
	Charity								
Occasional	Household Supplies								
	Personal								
	Clothes								
	Medical								
	School Exp.								
	Recreation								
	Counseling								
	Meals (Events)								
Installment	Credit Cards:								
	Visa								
	MC								
Total ③	Total Income								
	Total Exp. Excludes								
	Total Excess								
	Total Short								

MONTHLY BUDGET WORKSHEET   DECEMBER

					Checking Bal.				Reserve Savings
INCOME SOURCE									
① Net Income Total Amount									
	Expenses	① Amount	Date Due	Date Paid	Date ② Rcv.:				
Fixed Amounts	Mortgage/Rent								
	Car Payments								
	Other Loans:								
	Internet Access								
	Day Care								
	Insurance								
	Insurance								
	Clubs/Dues								
	Savings—Emergency								
	Savings—Goals								
	Savings—Reserve								
	Allowance								
Fixed Variable	Electricity								
	Heating Oil/Gas								
	Water								
	Garbage								
	Telephone/Cell Phone								
	Cable TV								
	Groceries								
	Meals Out								
	Auto/Gas								
	Auto								
	Child Allowance								
	Charity								
Occasional	Household Supplies								
	Personal								
	Clothes								
	Medical								
	School Exp.								
	Recreation								
	Counseling								
	Meals In (Books)								
Installment	Credit Cards:								
	Visa								
	MC								
Total	Total Income								
	Total Exp. Excludes								
	Total Excess								
	Total Short								

VARIABLE INCOME WORKSHEET

Income Source	Jan.	Feb.	Mar.	Apr.	May	June
INVESTMENT INCOME						
COMMISSIONS						
BONUS						
BUSINESS INCOME						
CONSULTANT						
REIMBURSEMENT						
FREELANCE						
ROYALTY						
OTHER*						
TOTAL INCOME						

* Tax refund, cash gifts, inheritance, trust, gratuities, rental property, insurance settlement, property sale, affiliate website sales, etc.

VARIABLE INCOME WORKSHEET

Income Source	July	Aug.	Sept.	Oct.	Nov.	Dec	Total
INVESTMENT INCOME							
COMMISSIONS							
BONUS							
BUSINESS INCOME							
CONSULTANT							
REIMBURSEMENT							
FREELANCE							
ROYALTY							
OTHER*							
TOTAL INCOME							

* Tax refund, cash gifts, inheritance, trust, gratuities, rental property, insurance settlement, property sale, affiliate website sales, etc.

BASIC MONTHLY HOUSEHOLD AND PERSONAL EXPENSES
(Refer to Monthly Budget Worksheet and Yearly Budget Worksheet for more comprehensive categories.)

Expenses	Jan.	Feb.	March	April	May	June
Est. Taxes						
Mortgage						
Car Payment						
Loans						
Insurance						
Utilities						
Phones						
Groceries						
Gas						
Credit Cards						
Major Periodic						
Total Expenses						
Total Inc. Pg 31-32						
Difference						
Deposit Save*						
Withdraw Save						

* If extra funds are available this month, see the Windfall Planner on page 35.

BASIC MONTHLY HOUSEHOLD AND PERSONAL EXPENSES
(Refer to Monthly Budget Worksheet and Yearly Budget Worksheet for more comprehensive categories.)

Expenses	July	Aug.	Sept.	Oct.	Nov.	Dec.	Total
Est. Taxes							
Mortgage							
Car Payment							
Loans							
Insurance							
Utilities							
Phones							
Groceries							
Gas							
Credit Cards							
Major Periodic							
Total Expenses							
Total Inc. Pg 31-32							
Difference							
Deposit Save							
Withdraw Save							

* If extra funds are available this month, see the Windfall Planner on page 35.

WINDFALL PLANNER

Date: _____
Source of Money: _____
Total Amount: _____

Possible Expense Item	Amount	or	Percent
Estimated Taxes to Put in Savings (if no taxes have been taken out)	$ _____		% _____
Catch Up on Payments Currently Behind	_____		_____
Back Taxes Still Due (federal, state, property)	_____		_____
Credit Card(s)–Pay Down or Off	_____		_____
Credit Card(s)–Pay Down or Off	_____		_____
Loan(s)–Pay Down or Off	_____		_____
Loan(s)–Pay Down or Off	_____		_____
Cover _____ No. of Months of Living Expenses	_____		_____
(Put this in savings.)	_____		_____
Stock Up on Household and/or Grocery Items	_____		_____
Upcoming Major Expense(s)	_____		_____
(See Yearly Budget Worksheet on p. 13)	_____		_____
Emergency Savings Account	_____		_____
Home Improvement Project(s)	_____		_____
New Purchases	_____		_____
Investments/Retirement/College	_____		_____
Vacation/Travel/Trips/Fun Money	_____		_____
Charitable Giving	_____		_____
Other	_____		_____
_____	_____		_____
_____	_____		_____
_____	_____		_____
_____	_____		_____
_____	_____		_____
GRAND TOTAL	$ _____		_____ %

DEBT PAYOFF RECORD

	LOANS					
CREDITOR						**Total***
Account Number						
Total Balance Due						
Phone Number						
Interest Rate (APR)						
January						
Amount Paid						
Interest/Penalty						
Balance Due						
February						
Amount Paid						
Interest/Penalty						
Balance Due						
March						
Amount Paid						
Interest/Penalty						
Balance Due						
April						
Amount Paid						
Interest/Penalty						
Balance Due						
May						
Amount Paid						
Interest/Penalty						
Balance Due						
June						
Amount Paid						
Interest/Penalty						
Balance Due						

DEBT PAYOFF RECORD CONT.

July						
Amount Paid						
Interest/Penalty						
Balance Due						
August						
Amount Paid						
Interest/Penalty						
Balance Due						
September						
Amount Paid						
Interest/Penalty						
Balance Due						
October						
Amount Paid						
Interest/Penalty						
Balance Due						
November						
Amount Paid						
Interest/Penalty						
Balance Due						
December						
Amount Paid						
Interest/Penalty						
Balance Due						
Balance Due						

* Add your total for loan debt to the Grand Total column on page 40.

DEBT PAYOFF RECORD

CREDIT CARDS						
CREDITOR						Total*
Account Number						
Total Balance Due						
Phone Number						
Interest Rate (APR)						
January						
Amount Paid						
Interest/Penalty						
Balance Due						
February						
Amount Paid						
Interest/Penalty						
Balance Due						
March						
Amount Paid						
Interest/Penalty						
Balance Due						
April						
Amount Paid						
Interest/Penalty						
Balance Due						
May						
Amount Paid						
Interest/Penalty						
Balance Due						
June						
Amount Paid						
Interest/Penalty						
Balance Due						
July						
Amount Paid						
Interest/Penalty						
Balance Due						

DEBT PAYOFF RECORD CONT.

August						
Amount Paid						
Interest/Penalty						
Balance Due						
September						
Amount Paid						
Interest/Penalty						
Balance Due						
October						
Amount Paid						
Interest/Penalty						
Balance Due						
November						
Amount Paid						
Interest/Penalty						
Balance Due						
December						
Amount Paid						
Interest/Penalty						
Balance Due						
Balance Due						

* Add your total for credit card debt to the Grand Total column on page 40.

DEBT PAYOFF RECORD

CREDITOR					Total	Grand Total
Account Number						
Total Balance Due						
Phone Number						
Interest Rate (APR)						
January						
Amount Paid						
Interest/Penalty						
Balance Due						
February						
Amount Paid						
Interest/Penalty						
Balance Due						
March						
Amount Paid						
Interest/Penalty						
Balance Due						
April						
Amount Paid						
Interest/Penalty						
Balance Due						
May						
Amount Paid						
Interest/Penalty						
Balance Due						
June						
Amount Paid						
Interest/Penalty						
Balance Due						

DEBT PAYOFF RECORD CONT.

July						
Amount Paid						
Interest/Penalty						
Balance Due						
August						
Amount Paid						
Interest/Penalty						
Balance Due						
September						
Amount Paid						
Interest/Penalty						
Balance Due						
October						
Amount Paid						
Interest/Penalty						
Balance Due						
November						
Amount Paid						
Interest/Penalty						
Balance Due						
December						
Amount Paid						
Interest/Penalty						
Balance Due						
Balance Due						

DEBT REPAYMENT WORKSHEET

Step 1 Disposable Income *

Total Amount of Disposable Income Available to Pay Off Debt: $ _____

(Calculate your budget on the **Monthly Budget Worksheet** beginning on page 70.) How much money is available to apply to debt?

The more you owe a creditor, the more money and higher percent you will pay them from your Disposable Income.

Step 2 Total Combined Debt **

Total Amount of All Debt Combined: $ _____

(Transfer the total from the **Debt Payoff Record** beginning on page 40.)

Step 3 New Payment ***

List below the total balances you owe each creditor listed on the **Debt Payoff Record**. Start with the smallest balance and then follow the formula below to determine the new payment for each creditor.

Creditor	Bala	÷	Total ** Combined	Share Percent (of Total	Disposabl	=	New Payment
Dentist	$500	÷	$11,500	4.3%	$700	=	$30.43
Visa	$1,500	÷	$11,500	13.0%	$700	=	$91.30
_____	_____		_____	_____	_____		_____
_____	_____		_____	_____	_____		_____
_____	_____		_____	_____	_____		_____
_____	_____		_____	_____	_____		_____
_____	_____		_____	_____	_____		_____
_____	_____		_____	_____	_____		_____
_____	_____		_____	_____	_____		_____
_____	_____		_____	_____	_____		_____
_____	_____		_____	_____	_____		_____
_____	_____		_____	_____	_____		_____
_____	_____		_____	_____	_____		_____
_____	_____		_____	_____	_____		_____
_____	_____		_____	_____	_____		_____
_____	_____		_____	_____	_____		_____

CREDIT CARD PURCHASE RECORD

SAMPLE

	JAN.		FEB.		MAR.		APR.		MAY		JUNE	
	Billing Cycle Closing Date: ① _____											
③	Item	Amount	Item	Amount	Item	Amount	Item	Amount	Item	Amount	Item	Amount
3/gas	②	14.91										
7/Shoes		20.82										
	Total											

ONLINE/ELECTRONIC CONNECTION TO THE BUDGET KIT

Online Bill Payments

If you don't want to list your charges on this worksheet, you can register online at your credit card company's website and see your current charges and balance due. As you fill in the "Installment" blanks of the **Monthly Budget Worksheet** to plan out your bills, you will know exactly how much to anticipate for your credit card payments. When your bill arrives, you can still pay by check or pay the bill directly online from your checking account, using either the credit card website or your bank's website.

Online Budget Programs

Coordinating credit card charges with a monthly budget accurately and effectively is probably one of the more challenging steps depending on your online budget program, credit card debt situation, and level of sophistication. Even the manual approach to this process gets confusing for many people. See if your online budget program has a way to link a credit card charge in a particular category with the same category in your outlined budget for the month and then has a way to plan the payment. Not all programs are designed to coordinate this process.

The more popular online budget programs like Quicken (Mint) will have well-designed systems for virtually coordinating the credit card charges with the monthly budget and then including a virtual transfer for the payment plan. If you are a heavy credit card user, be sure this feature is offered with the online program you are using and is easy to use.

CREDIT CARD PURCHASE RECORD

		JAN.		FEB.		MAR.		APR.		MAY		JUNE
Billing Cycle Closing Date:												
Item	A	Item	A	Item	A	Item	A	Item	A	Item	A	
Total												

CREDIT CARD PURCHASE RECORD CONT.

		JULY		AUG.		SEPT.		OCT.		NOV.		DEC.	
Billing Cycle Closing Date:													
Item	A	Item	A	Item	A	Item	A	Item	A	Item	A	Item	A
Total													

MONTHLY EXPENSE RECORD

Balance Forward from Last Month:
Cash: _____ Checking: _____ Savings: _____

NET INCOME

SALARY/COMMISSIONS			TOTAL
		TOTAL INCOME	
OTHER			
		Subtotal Other Income	
		TOTAL NET INCOME	

SAVINGS

(Describe)	
TOTAL SAVINGS	

INVESTMENTS/RETIREMENT

TOTAL INVESTMENTS/RETIREMENT	

		FOOD			HOUSEHOLD				TRANSPORTATION			PERSONAL		HEALTH	
		groceries	cafeteria fast food dining out school lunches	tobacco alcohol snacks beverages water	cleaner mainten. house yard pool	appliances furniture furnishings supplies	postage copies ATM fees bank fees misc.	interest taxes	gas	auto mainten. wash license	taxi transit tolls/passes parking	clothing alterations dry clean. laundry shoe care	toiletries cosmetics hair nails massage	doctor dentist vision medicine vitamins	personal growth therapy
WEEK 1	1														
	2														
	3														
	4														
	5														
	6														
	7														
WEEK 2	8														
	9														
	10														
	11														
	12														
	13														
	14														
WEEK 3	15														
	16														
	17														
	18														
	19														
	20														
	21														
WEEK 4	22														
	23														
	24														
	25														
	26														
	27														
	28														
	29														
	30														
	31														
	T*														
	B*														
	D*														

* T = Total; B = Budget; D = Difference

MONTHLY EXPENSE RECORD

JANUARY

FIXED EXPENSES

Monthly	Amount	Monthly	Amount
Mortgage/Rent		Insurance:	
Assn. Fee		House/Apt	
Heating Oil/Gas		Auto	
Electricity		Life	
Water/Refuse		Health	
Garbage/Sewer		Dental	
Telephone		Disability	
Cellular Phone		Long Term	
Cable/Satellite/TiVo			
Internet			
Child Support			
Spousal Support			
		TOTAL FIXED EXPENSES	

INSTALLMENT EXPENSES

Loans/Credit Cards	Amount
TOTAL	

TOTAL EXPENSES

Total Fixed Expenses	
Total Installment Expenses	
Total Monthly Expenses from Below	
GRAND TOTAL EXPENSES	
Plus Amount Paid to Savings	

		RECREATION/ENTERTAINMENT/EDUCATION					FAMILY			GENERAL					
	vacation trips	entertain. DVD movies music parties	lottery sports hobbies lessons clubs	computer upgrades software supplies service	seminar workshop tuition supplies	newspaper books magazines software games/apps	elder care child care sitter tutor	infant exp. allowance school exp. toys arcades	pet vet supplies services sitter	gifts cards flowers	charitable contribut. church temple	work expense dues reimburse- ments	prof. services legal CPA investment	other (add explanation)	
WEEK 1	1														
	2														
	3														
	4														
	5														
	6														
	7														
WEEK 2	8														
	9														
	10														
	11														
	12														
	13														
	14														
WEEK 3	15														
	16														
	17														
	18														
	19														
	20														
	21														
WEEK 4	22														
	23														
	24														
	25														
	26														
	27														
	28														
	29														
	30														
	31														
	T*														
	B*														
	D*														

* T = Total; B = Budget; D = Difference

MONTHLY EXPENSE RECORD

Balance Forward from Last Month:
Cash: _____ Checking: _____ Savings: _____

NET INCOME

SALARY/COMMISSIONS			TOTAL
		TOTAL INCOME	
OTHER			
		Subtotal Other Income	
		TOTAL NET INCOME	

SAVINGS

(Describe)	
TOTAL SAVINGS	

INVESTMENTS/RETIREMENT

TOTAL INVESTMENTS/RETIREMENT	

	FOOD			HOUSEHOLD				TRANSPORTATION			PERSONAL		HEALTH	
	groceries	cafeteria fast food dining out school lunches	tobacco alcohol snacks beverages water	cleaner mainten. house yard pool	appliances furniture furnishings supplies	postage copies ATM fees bank fees misc.	interest taxes	gas	auto mainten. wash license	taxi transit tolls/passes parking	clothing alterations dry clean. laundry shoe care	toiletries cosmetics hair nails massage	doctor dentist vision medicine vitamins	personal growth therapy
WEEK 1 1														
2														
3														
4														
5														
6														
7														
WEEK 2 8														
9														
10														
11														
12														
13														
14														
WEEK 3 15														
16														
17														
18														
19														
20														
21														
WEEK 4 22														
23														
24														
25														
26														
27														
28														
29														
30														
31														
T*														
B*														
D*														

* T = Total; B = Budget; D = Difference

MONTHLY EXPENSE RECORD

FEBRUARY

FIXED EXPENSES

Monthly	Amount	Monthly	Amount
Mortgage/Rent		Insurance:	
Assn. Fee		House/Apt	
Heating Oil/Gas		Auto	
Electricity		Life	
Water/Refuse		Health	
Garbage/Sewer		Dental	
Telephone		Disability	
Cellular Phone		Long Term	
Cable/Satellite/TiVo			
Internet			
Child Support			
Spousal Support			
		TOTAL FIXED EXPENSES	

INSTALLMENT EXPENSES

Loans/Credit Cards	Amount
TOTAL	

TOTAL EXPENSES

Total Fixed Expenses	
Total Installment Expenses	
Total Monthly Expenses from Below	
GRAND TOTAL EXPENSES	
Plus Amount Paid to Savings	

RECREATION/ENTERTAINMENT/EDUCATION / FAMILY / GENERAL

		vacation trips	entertain. DVD movies music parties	lottery sports hobbies lessons clubs	computer upgrades software supplies service	seminar workshop tuition supplies	newspaper books magazines software games/apps	elder care child care sitter tutor	infant exp. allowance school exp. toys arcades	pet vet supplies services sitter	gifts cards flowers	charitable contribut. church temple	work expense dues reimbursements	prof. services legal CPA investment	other (add explanation)
W E E K 1	1														
	2														
	3														
	4														
	5														
	6														
	7														
W E E K 2	8														
	9														
	10														
	11														
	12														
	13														
	14														
W E E K 3	15														
	16														
	17														
	18														
	19														
	20														
	21														
W E E K 4	22														
	23														
	24														
	25														
	26														
	27														
	28														
	29														
	30														
	31														
	T*														
	B*														
	D*														

* T = Total; B = Budget; D = Difference

MONTHLY EXPENSE RECORD

Balance Forward from Last Month:
Cash: _____   Checking: _____   Savings: _____

NET INCOME

		TOTAL
SALARY/COMMISSIONS		
	TOTAL INCOME	
OTHER		
	Subtotal Other Income	
	TOTAL NET INCOME	

SAVINGS

(Describe)	
TOTAL SAVINGS	

INVESTMENTS/RETIREMENT

TOTAL INVESTMENTS/RETIREMENT	

	FOOD			HOUSEHOLD				TRANSPORTATION			PERSONAL		HEALTH	
	groceries	cafeteria fast food dining out school lunches	tobacco alcohol snacks beverages water	cleaner mainten. house yard pool	appliances furniture furnishings supplies	postage copies ATM fees bank fees misc.	interest taxes	gas	auto mainten. wash license	taxi transit tolls/passes parking	clothing alterations dry clean. laundry shoe care	toiletries cosmetics hair nails massage	doctor dentist vision medicine vitamins	personal growth therapy

WEEK 1: days 1–7
WEEK 2: days 8–14
WEEK 3: days 15–21
WEEK 4: days 22–31

T*
B*
D*

* T = Total; B = Budget; D = Difference

MONTHLY EXPENSE RECORD

MARCH

FIXED EXPENSES

Monthly	Amount	Monthly	Amount
Mortgage/Rent		Insurance:	
Assn. Fee		House/Apt	
Heating Oil/Gas		Auto	
Electricity		Life	
Water/Refuse		Health	
Garbage/Sewer		Dental	
Telephone		Disability	
Cellular Phone		Long Term	
Cable/Satellite/TiVo			
Internet			
Child Support			
Spousal Support			
		TOTAL FIXED EXPENSES	

INSTALLMENT EXPENSES

Loans/Credit Cards	Amount
TOTAL	

TOTAL EXPENSES

Total Fixed Expenses	
Total Installment Expenses	
Total Monthly Expenses from Below	
GRAND TOTAL EXPENSES	
Plus Amount Paid to Savings	

	RECREATION/ENTERTAINMENT/EDUCATION						FAMILY			GENERAL				
	vacation trips	entertain. DVD movies music parties	lottery sports hobbies lessons clubs	computer upgrades software supplies service	seminar workshop tuition supplies	newspaper books magazines software games/apps	elder care child care sitter tutor	infant exp. allowance school exp. toys arcades	pet vet supplies services sitter	gifts cards flowers	charitable contribut. church temple	work expense dues reimburse-ments	prof. services legal CPA investment	other (add explanation)
WEEK 1 — 1–7														
WEEK 2 — 8–14														
WEEK 3 — 15–21														
WEEK 4 — 22–31														
T*														
B*														
D*														

* T = Total; B = Budget; D = Difference

MONTHLY EXPENSE RECORD

Balance Forward from Last Month:
Cash: _____ Checking: _____ Savings: _____

NET INCOME

SALARY/COMMISSIONS			TOTAL
		TOTAL INCOME	
OTHER			
		Subtotal Other Income	
		TOTAL NET INCOME	

SAVINGS

(Describe)	
TOTAL SAVINGS	

INVESTMENTS/RETIREMENT

TOTAL INVESTMENTS/RETIREMENT	

	FOOD			HOUSEHOLD				TRANSPORTATION			PERSONAL		HEALTH	
	groceries	cafeteria fast food dining out school lunches	tobacco alcohol snacks beverages water	cleaner mainten. house yard pool	appliances furniture furnishings supplies	postage copies ATM fees bank fees misc.	interest taxes	gas	auto mainten. wash license	taxi transit tolls/passes parking	clothing alterations dry clean. laundry shoe care	toiletries cosmetics hair nails massage	doctor dentist vision medicine vitamins	personal growth therapy
WEEK 1 (1–7)														
WEEK 2 (8–14)														
WEEK 3 (15–21)														
WEEK 4 (22–31)														
T*														
B*														
D*														

* T = Total; B = Budget; D = Difference

MONTHLY EXPENSE RECORD

APRIL

FIXED EXPENSES

Monthly	Amount	Monthly	Amount
Mortgage/Rent		Insurance:	
Assn. Fee		House/Apt	
Heating Oil/Gas		Auto	
Electricity		Life	
Water/Refuse		Health	
Garbage/Sewer		Dental	
Telephone		Disability	
Cellular Phone		Long Term	
Cable/Satellite/TiVo			
Internet			
Child Support			
Spousal Support			
		TOTAL FIXED EXPENSES	

INSTALLMENT EXPENSES

Loans/Credit Cards	Amount
TOTAL	

TOTAL EXPENSES

Total Fixed Expenses	
Total Installment Expenses	
Total Monthly Expenses from Below	
GRAND TOTAL EXPENSES	
Plus Amount Paid to Savings	

Weekly Expense Log

		RECREATION/ENTERTAINMENT/EDUCATION					FAMILY				GENERAL			
	vacation trips	entertain. DVD movies music parties	lottery sports hobbies lessons clubs	computer upgrades software supplies service	seminar workshop tuition supplies	newspaper books magazines software games/apps	elder care child care sitter tutor	infant exp. allowance school exp. toys arcades	pet vet supplies services sitter	gifts cards flowers	charitable contribut. church temple	work expense dues reimburse- ments	prof. services legal CPA investment	other (add explanation)
WEEK 1 1														
2														
3														
4														
5														
6														
7														
WEEK 2 8														
9														
10														
11														
12														
13														
14														
WEEK 3 15														
16														
17														
18														
19														
20														
21														
WEEK 4 22														
23														
24														
25														
26														
27														
28														
29														
30														
31														
T*														
B*														
D*														

* T = Total; B = Budget; D = Difference

MONTHLY EXPENSE RECORD

Balance Forward from Last Month:
Cash: _____ Checking: _____ Savings: _____

NET INCOME

SALARY/COMMISSIONS			TOTAL
		TOTAL INCOME	
OTHER			
		Subtotal Other Income	
		TOTAL NET INCOME	

SAVINGS

(Describe)	
TOTAL SAVINGS	

INVESTMENTS/RETIREMENT

TOTAL INVESTMENTS/RETIREMENT	

	FOOD			HOUSEHOLD				TRANSPORTATION			PERSONAL		HEALTH	
	groceries	cafeteria / fast food / dining out / school lunches	tobacco / alcohol / snacks / beverages / water	cleaner / mainten. / house / yard / pool	appliances / furniture / furnishings / supplies	postage / copies / ATM fees / bank fees / misc.	interest / taxes	gas	auto / mainten. / wash / license	taxi / transit / tolls/passes / parking	clothing / alterations / dry clean. / laundry / shoe care	toiletries / cosmetics / hair / nails / massage	doctor / dentist / vision / medicine / vitamins	personal growth / therapy

WEEK 1 (days 1–7)

WEEK 2 (days 8–14)

WEEK 3 (days 15–21)

WEEK 4 (days 22–31)

T* B* D*

* T = Total; B = Budget; D = Difference

MONTHLY EXPENSE RECORD

MAY

FIXED EXPENSES

Monthly	Amount	Monthly	Amount
Mortgage/Rent		Insurance:	
Assn. Fee		House/Apt	
Heating Oil/Gas		Auto	
Electricity		Life	
Water/Refuse		Health	
Garbage/Sewer		Dental	
Telephone		Disability	
Cellular Phone		Long Term	
Cable/Satellite/TiVo			
Internet			
Child Support			
Spousal Support			
		TOTAL FIXED EXPENSES	

INSTALLMENT EXPENSES

Loans/Credit Cards	Amount
TOTAL	

TOTAL EXPENSES

Total Fixed Expenses	
Total Installment Expenses	
Total Monthly Expenses from Below	
GRAND TOTAL EXPENSES	
Plus Amount Paid to Savings	

		RECREATION/ENTERTAINMENT/EDUCATION					FAMILY			GENERAL				
	vacation trips	entertain. DVD movies music parties	lottery sports hobbies lessons clubs	computer upgrades software supplies service	seminar workshop tuition supplies	newspaper books magazines software games/apps	elder care child care sitter tutor	infant exp. allowance school exp. toys arcades	pet vet supplies services sitter	gifts cards flowers	charitable contribut. church temple	work expense dues reimbursements	prof. services legal CPA investment	other (add explanation)
WEEK 1 — 1														
2														
3														
4														
5														
6														
7														
WEEK 2 — 8														
9														
10														
11														
12														
13														
14														
WEEK 3 — 15														
16														
17														
18														
19														
20														
21														
WEEK 4 — 22														
23														
24														
25														
26														
27														
28														
29														
30														
31														
T*														
B*														
D*														

* T = Total; B = Budget; D = Difference

MONTHLY EXPENSE RECORD

Balance Forward from Last Month:
Cash: _____ Checking: _____ Savings: _____

NET INCOME

			TOTAL
SALARY/COMMISSIONS			
		TOTAL INCOME	
OTHER			
		Subtotal Other Income	
		TOTAL NET INCOME	

SAVINGS

(Describe)	
	TOTAL SAVINGS

INVESTMENTS/RETIREMENT

	TOTAL INVESTMENTS/RETIREMENT

	FOOD			HOUSEHOLD					TRANSPORTATION			PERSONAL		HEALTH	
	groceries	cafeteria fast food dining out school lunches	tobacco alcohol snacks beverages water	cleaner mainten. house yard pool	appliances furniture furnishings supplies	postage copies ATM fees bank fees misc.	interest taxes	gas	auto mainten. wash license	taxi transit tolls/passes parking	clothing alterations dry clean. laundry shoe care	toiletries cosmetics hair nails massage	doctor dentist vision medicine vitamins	personal growth therapy
WEEK 1 — 1														
2														
3														
4														
5														
6														
7														
WEEK 2 — 8														
9														
10														
11														
12														
13														
14														
WEEK 3 — 15														
16														
17														
18														
19														
20														
21														
WEEK 4 — 22														
23														
24														
25														
26														
27														
28														
29														
30														
31														
T*														
B*														
D*														

* T = Total; B = Budget; D = Difference

MONTHLY EXPENSE RECORD

JUNE

FIXED EXPENSES

Monthly	Amount	Monthly	Amount
Mortgage/Rent		Insurance:	
Assn. Fee		House/Apt	
Heating Oil/Gas		Auto	
Electricity		Life	
Water/Refuse		Health	
Garbage/Sewer		Dental	
Telephone		Disability	
Cellular Phone		Long Term	
Cable/Satellite/TiVo			
Internet			
Child Support			
Spousal Support			
		TOTAL FIXED EXPENSES	

INSTALLMENT EXPENSES

Loans/Credit Cards	Amount
TOTAL	

TOTAL EXPENSES

Total Fixed Expenses	
Total Installment Expenses	
Total Monthly Expenses from Below	
GRAND TOTAL EXPENSES	
Plus Amount Paid to Savings	

	RECREATION/ENTERTAINMENT/EDUCATION						FAMILY			GENERAL				
	vacation trips	entertain. DVD movies music parties	lottery sports hobbies lessons clubs	computer upgrades software supplies service	seminar workshop tuition supplies	newspaper books magazines software games/apps	elder care child care sitter tutor	infant exp. allowance school exp. toys arcades	pet vet supplies services sitter	gifts cards flowers	charitable contribut. church temple	work expense dues reimburse- ments	prof. services legal CPA investment	other (add explanation)
WEEK 1 — 1														
2														
3														
4														
5														
6														
7														
WEEK 2 — 8														
9														
10														
11														
12														
13														
14														
WEEK 3 — 15														
16														
17														
18														
19														
20														
21														
WEEK 4 — 22														
23														
24														
25														
26														
27														
28														
29														
30														
31														
T*														
B*														
D*														

* T = Total; B = Budget; D = Difference

MONTHLY EXPENSE RECORD

Balance Forward from Last Month:
Cash: _____ Checking: _____ Savings: _____

NET INCOME

SALARY/COMMISSIONS			TOTAL
		TOTAL INCOME	
OTHER			
	Subtotal Other Income		
	TOTAL NET INCOME		

SAVINGS

(Describe)	
TOTAL SAVINGS	

INVESTMENTS/RETIREMENT

TOTAL INVESTMENTS/RETIREMENT	

		FOOD		HOUSEHOLD			TRANSPORTATION			PERSONAL		HEALTH	
	groceries	cafeteria fast food dining out school lunches	tobacco alcohol snacks beverages water	cleaner mainten. house yard pool	appliances furniture furnishings supplies	postage copies ATM fees bank fees misc.	interest taxes	gas	auto mainten. wash license	taxi transit tolls/passes parking	clothing alterations dry clean. laundry shoe care	toiletries cosmetics hair nails massage	doctor dentist vision medicine vitamins	personal growth therapy
WEEK 1 (1–7)														
WEEK 2 (8–14)														
WEEK 3 (15–21)														
WEEK 4 (22–31)														
T*														
B*														
D*														

* T = Total; B = Budget; D = Difference

MONTHLY EXPENSE RECORD

JULY

FIXED EXPENSES

Monthly	Amount	Monthly	Amount
Mortgage/Rent		Insurance:	
Assn. Fee		House/Apt	
Heating Oil/Gas		Auto	
Electricity		Life	
Water/Refuse		Health	
Garbage/Sewer		Dental	
Telephone		Disability	
Cellular Phone		Long Term	
Cable/Satellite/TiVo			
Internet			
Child Support			
Spousal Support			
		TOTAL FIXED EXPENSES	

INSTALLMENT EXPENSES

Loans/Credit Cards	Amount
TOTAL	

TOTAL EXPENSES

Total Fixed Expenses	
Total Installment Expenses	
Total Monthly Expenses from Below	
GRAND TOTAL EXPENSES	
Plus Amount Paid to Savings	

		RECREATION/ENTERTAINMENT/EDUCATION					FAMILY			GENERAL				
	vacation trips	entertain. DVD movies music parties	lottery sports hobbies lessons clubs	computer upgrades software supplies service	seminar workshop tuition supplies	newspaper books magazines software games/apps	elder care child care sitter tutor	infant exp. allowance school exp. toys arcades	pet vet supplies services sitter	gifts cards flowers	charitable contribut. church temple	work expense dues reimburse- ments	prof. services legal CPA investment	other (add explanation)
WEEK 1 — 1														
2														
3														
4														
5														
6														
7														
WEEK 2 — 8														
9														
10														
11														
12														
13														
14														
WEEK 3 — 15														
16														
17														
18														
19														
20														
21														
WEEK 4 — 22														
23														
24														
25														
26														
27														
28														
29														
30														
31														
T*														
B*														
D*														

* T = Total; B = Budget; D = Difference

MONTHLY EXPENSE RECORD

Balance Forward from Last Month:
Cash: _____ Checking: _____ Savings: _____

NET INCOME

			TOTAL
SALARY/COMMISSIONS			
		TOTAL INCOME	
OTHER			
		Subtotal Other Income	
		TOTAL NET INCOME	

SAVINGS

(Describe)	
TOTAL SAVINGS	

INVESTMENTS/RETIREMENT

TOTAL INVESTMENTS/RETIREMENT	

	FOOD			HOUSEHOLD					TRANSPORTATION			PERSONAL		HEALTH	
	groceries	cafeteria fast food dining out school lunches	tobacco alcohol snacks beverages water	cleaner mainten. house yard pool	appliances furniture furnishings supplies	postage copies ATM fees bank fees misc.	interest taxes	gas	auto mainten. wash license	taxi transit tolls/passes parking	clothing alterations dry clean. laundry shoe care	toiletries cosmetics hair nails massage	doctor dentist vision medicine vitamins	personal growth therapy
WEEK 1 — 1														
2														
3														
4														
5														
6														
7														
WEEK 2 — 8														
9														
10														
11														
12														
13														
14														
WEEK 3 — 15														
16														
17														
18														
19														
20														
21														
WEEK 4 — 22														
23														
24														
25														
26														
27														
28														
29														
30														
31														
T*														
B*														
D*														

* T = Total; B = Budget; D = Difference

MONTHLY EXPENSE RECORD

AUGUST

FIXED EXPENSES

Monthly	Amount	Monthly	Amount
Mortgage/Rent		Insurance:	
Assn. Fee		House/Apt	
Heating Oil/Gas		Auto	
Electricity		Life	
Water/Refuse		Health	
Garbage/Sewer		Dental	
Telephone		Disability	
Cellular Phone		Long Term	
Cable/Satellite/TiVo			
Internet			
Child Support			
Spousal Support			
		TOTAL FIXED EXPENSES	

INSTALLMENT EXPENSES

Loans/Credit Cards	Amount
TOTAL	

TOTAL EXPENSES

Total Fixed Expenses	
Total Installment Expenses	
Total Monthly Expenses from Below	
GRAND TOTAL EXPENSES	
Plus Amount Paid to Savings	

RECREATION/ENTERTAINMENT/EDUCATION — FAMILY — GENERAL

		vacation trips	entertain. DVD movies music parties	lottery sports hobbies lessons clubs	computer upgrades software supplies service	seminar workshop tuition supplies	newspaper books magazines software games/apps	elder care child care sitter tutor	infant exp. allowance school exp. toys arcades	pet vet supplies services sitter	gifts cards flowers	charitable contribut. church temple	work expense dues reimbursements	prof. services legal CPA investment	other (add explanation)
W E E K 1	1														
	2														
	3														
	4														
	5														
	6														
	7														
W E E K 2	8														
	9														
	10														
	11														
	12														
	13														
	14														
W E E K 3	15														
	16														
	17														
	18														
	19														
	20														
	21														
W E E K 4	22														
	23														
	24														
	25														
	26														
	27														
	28														
	29														
	30														
	31														
	T*														
	B*														
	D*														

* T = Total; B = Budget; D = Difference

MONTHLY EXPENSE RECORD

Balance Forward from Last Month:
Cash: _____ Checking: _____ Savings: _____

NET INCOME

SALARY/COMMISSIONS			TOTAL
		TOTAL INCOME	
OTHER			
		Subtotal Other Income	
		TOTAL NET INCOME	

SAVINGS

(Describe)	
TOTAL SAVINGS	

INVESTMENTS/RETIREMENT

TOTAL INVESTMENTS/RETIREMENT	

	FOOD			HOUSEHOLD				TRANSPORTATION			PERSONAL		HEALTH	
	groceries	cafeteria fast food dining out school lunches	tobacco alcohol snacks beverages water	cleaner mainten. house yard pool	appliances furniture furnishings supplies	postage copies ATM fees bank fees misc.	interest taxes	gas	auto mainten. wash license	taxi transit tolls/passes parking	clothing alterations dry clean. laundry shoe care	toiletries cosmetics hair nails massage	doctor dentist vision medicine vitamins	personal growth therapy

WEEK 1 (rows 1–7)

WEEK 2 (rows 8–14)

WEEK 3 (rows 15–21)

WEEK 4 (rows 22–31)

T*
B*
D*

* T = Total; B = Budget; D = Difference

MONTHLY EXPENSE RECORD

SEPTEMBER

FIXED EXPENSES

Monthly	Amount	Monthly	Amount
Mortgage/Rent		Insurance:	
Assn. Fee		House/Apt	
Heating Oil/Gas		Auto	
Electricity		Life	
Water/Refuse		Health	
Garbage/Sewer		Dental	
Telephone		Disability	
Cellular Phone		Long Term	
Cable/Satellite/TiVo			
Internet			
Child Support			
Spousal Support			
		TOTAL FIXED EXPENSES	

INSTALLMENT EXPENSES

Loans/Credit Cards	Amount
TOTAL	

TOTAL EXPENSES

Total Fixed Expenses	
Total Installment Expenses	
Total Monthly Expenses from Below	
GRAND TOTAL EXPENSES	
Plus Amount Paid to Savings	

		RECREATION/ENTERTAINMENT/EDUCATION					FAMILY			GENERAL				
		vacation trips	entertain. DVD movies music parties	lottery sports hobbies lessons clubs	computer upgrades software supplies service	seminar workshop tuition supplies	newspaper books magazines software games/apps	elder care child care sitter tutor	infant exp. allowance school exp. toys arcades	pet vet supplies services sitter	gifts cards flowers	charitable contribut. church temple	work expense dues reimbursements	prof. services legal CPA investment	other (add explanation)
WEEK 1	1														
	2														
	3														
	4														
	5														
	6														
	7														
WEEK 2	8														
	9														
	10														
	11														
	12														
	13														
	14														
WEEK 3	15														
	16														
	17														
	18														
	19														
	20														
	21														
WEEK 4	22														
	23														
	24														
	25														
	26														
	27														
	28														
	29														
	30														
	31														
	T*														
	B*														
	D*														

* T = Total; B = Budget; D = Difference

MONTHLY EXPENSE RECORD

Balance Forward from Last Month:
Cash: _____ Checking: _____ Savings: _____

NET INCOME

SALARY/COMMISSIONS			TOTAL
		TOTAL INCOME	
OTHER			
		Subtotal Other Income	
		TOTAL NET INCOME	

SAVINGS

(Describe)	
TOTAL SAVINGS	

INVESTMENTS/RETIREMENT

TOTAL INVESTMENTS/RETIREMENT	

	FOOD			HOUSEHOLD					TRANSPORTATION			PERSONAL		HEALTH	
	groceries	cafeteria fast food dining out school lunches	tobacco alcohol snacks beverages water	cleaner mainten. house yard pool	appliances furniture furnishings supplies	postage copies ATM fees bank fees misc.	interest taxes	gas	auto mainten. wash license	taxi transit tolls/passes parking	clothing alterations dry clean. laundry shoe care	toiletries cosmetics hair nails massage	doctor dentist vision medicine vitamins	personal growth therapy

WEEK 1 (days 1–7)

WEEK 2 (days 8–14)

WEEK 3 (days 15–21)

WEEK 4 (days 22–31)

T*
B*
D*

* T = Total; B = Budget; D = Difference

MONTHLY EXPENSE RECORD

OCTOBER

FIXED EXPENSES

Monthly	Amount	Monthly	Amount
Mortgage/Rent		Insurance:	
Assn. Fee		House/Apt	
Heating Oil/Gas		Auto	
Electricity		Life	
Water/Refuse		Health	
Garbage/Sewer		Dental	
Telephone		Disability	
Cellular Phone		Long Term	
Cable/Satellite/TiVo			
Internet			
Child Support			
Spousal Support			
		TOTAL FIXED EXPENSES	

INSTALLMENT EXPENSES

Loans/Credit Cards	Amount
TOTAL	

TOTAL EXPENSES

Total Fixed Expenses	
Total Installment Expenses	
Total Monthly Expenses from Below	
GRAND TOTAL EXPENSES	
Plus Amount Paid to Savings	

		RECREATION/ENTERTAINMENT/EDUCATION					FAMILY			GENERAL				
	vacation trips	entertain. DVD movies music parties	lottery sports hobbies lessons clubs	computer upgrades software supplies service	seminar workshop tuition supplies	newspaper books magazines software games/apps	elder care child care sitter tutor	infant exp. allowance school exp. toys arcades	pet vet supplies services sitter	gifts cards flowers	charitable contribut. church temple	work expense dues reimburse-ments	prof. services legal CPA investment	other (add explanation)
WEEK 1	1													
	2													
	3													
	4													
	5													
	6													
	7													
WEEK 2	8													
	9													
	10													
	11													
	12													
	13													
	14													
WEEK 3	15													
	16													
	17													
	18													
	19													
	20													
	21													
WEEK 4	22													
	23													
	24													
	25													
	26													
	27													
	28													
	29													
	30													
	31													
	T*													
	B*													
	D*													

* T = Total; B = Budget; D = Difference

MONTHLY EXPENSE RECORD

Balance Forward from Last Month:
Cash: _____ Checking: _____ Savings: _____

NET INCOME

SALARY/COMMISSIONS		TOTAL
	TOTAL INCOME	
OTHER		
	Subtotal Other Income	
	TOTAL NET INCOME	

SAVINGS

(Describe)	
	TOTAL SAVINGS

INVESTMENTS/RETIREMENT

	TOTAL INVESTMENTS/RETIREMENT

		FOOD			HOUSEHOLD				TRANSPORTATION			PERSONAL		HEALTH	
		groceries	cafeteria fast food dining out school lunches	tobacco alcohol snacks beverages water	cleaner mainten. house yard pool	appliances furniture furnishings supplies	postage copies ATM fees bank fees misc.	interest taxes	gas	auto mainten. wash license	taxi transit tolls/passes parking	clothing alterations dry clean. laundry shoe care	toiletries cosmetics hair nails massage	doctor dentist vision medicine vitamins	personal growth therapy
WEEK 1	1														
	2														
	3														
	4														
	5														
	6														
	7														
WEEK 2	8														
	9														
	10														
	11														
	12														
	13														
	14														
WEEK 3	15														
	16														
	17														
	18														
	19														
	20														
	21														
WEEK 4	22														
	23														
	24														
	25														
	26														
	27														
	28														
	29														
	30														
	31														
	T*														
	B*														
	D*														

* T = Total; B = Budget; D = Difference

MONTHLY EXPENSE RECORD

NOVEMBER

FIXED EXPENSES

Monthly	Amount	Monthly	Amount
Mortgage/Rent		Insurance:	
Assn. Fee		House/Apt	
Heating Oil/Gas		Auto	
Electricity		Life	
Water/Refuse		Health	
Garbage/Sewer		Dental	
Telephone		Disability	
Cellular Phone		Long Term	
Cable/Satellite/TiVo			
Internet			
Child Support			
Spousal Support			
		TOTAL FIXED EXPENSES	

INSTALLMENT EXPENSES

Loans/Credit Cards	Amount
TOTAL	

TOTAL EXPENSES

Total Fixed Expenses	
Total Installment Expenses	
Total Monthly Expenses from Below	
GRAND TOTAL EXPENSES	
Plus Amount Paid to Savings	

		RECREATION/ENTERTAINMENT/EDUCATION					FAMILY				GENERAL			
	vacation trips	entertain. DVD movies music parties	lottery sports hobbies lessons clubs	computer upgrades software supplies service	seminar workshop tuition supplies	newspaper books magazines software games/apps	elder care child care sitter tutor	infant exp. allowance school exp. toys arcades	pet vet supplies services sitter	gifts cards flowers	charitable contribut. church temple	work expense dues reimburse-ments	prof. services legal CPA investment	other (add explanation)
WEEK 1	1													
	2													
	3													
	4													
	5													
	6													
	7													
WEEK 2	8													
	9													
	10													
	11													
	12													
	13													
	14													
WEEK 3	15													
	16													
	17													
	18													
	19													
	20													
	21													
WEEK 4	22													
	23													
	24													
	25													
	26													
	27													
	28													
	29													
	30													
	31													
	T*													
	B*													
	D*													

* T = Total; B = Budget; D = Difference

MONTHLY EXPENSE RECORD

Balance Forward from Last Month:
Cash: _____ Checking: _____ Savings: _____

NET INCOME

			TOTAL
SALARY/COMMISSIONS			
	TOTAL INCOME		
OTHER			
	Subtotal Other Income		
	TOTAL NET INCOME		

SAVINGS

(Describe)	
TOTAL SAVINGS	

INVESTMENTS/RETIREMENT

TOTAL INVESTMENTS/RETIREMENT	

		FOOD			HOUSEHOLD				TRANSPORTATION			PERSONAL		HEALTH	
		groceries	cafeteria fast food dining out school lunches	tobacco alcohol snacks beverages water	cleaner mainten. house yard pool	appliances furniture furnishings supplies	postage copies ATM fees bank fees misc.	interest taxes	gas	auto mainten. wash license	taxi transit tolls/passes parking	clothing alterations dry clean. laundry shoe care	toiletries cosmetics hair nails massage	doctor dentist vision medicine vitamins	personal growth therapy
WEEK 1	1														
	2														
	3														
	4														
	5														
	6														
	7														
WEEK 2	8														
	9														
	10														
	11														
	12														
	13														
	14														
WEEK 3	15														
	16														
	17														
	18														
	19														
	20														
	21														
WEEK 4	22														
	23														
	24														
	25														
	26														
	27														
	28														
	29														
	30														
	31														
	T*														
	B*														
	D*														

* T = Total; B = Budget; D = Difference

MONTHLY EXPENSE RECORD

DECEMBER

FIXED EXPENSES

Monthly	Amount	Monthly	Amount
Mortgage/Rent		Insurance:	
Assn. Fee		House/Apt	
Heating Oil/Gas		Auto	
Electricity		Life	
Water/Refuse		Health	
Garbage/Sewer		Dental	
Telephone		Disability	
Cellular Phone		Long Term	
Cable/Satellite/TiVo			
Internet			
Child Support			
Spousal Support			
		TOTAL FIXED EXPENSES	

INSTALLMENT EXPENSES

Loans/Credit Cards	Amount
TOTAL	

TOTAL EXPENSES

Total Fixed Expenses	
Total Installment Expenses	
Total Monthly Expenses from Below	
GRAND TOTAL EXPENSES	
Plus Amount Paid to Savings	

		RECREATION/ENTERTAINMENT/EDUCATION						FAMILY				GENERAL			
	vacation trips	entertain. DVD movies music parties	lottery sports hobbies lessons clubs	computer upgrades software supplies service	seminar workshop tuition supplies	newspaper books magazines software games/apps	elder care child care sitter tutor	infant exp. allowance school exp. toys arcades	pet vet supplies services sitter	gifts cards flowers	charitable contribut. church temple	work expense dues reimburse-ments	prof. services legal CPA investment	other (add explanation)	
W E E K 1	1														
	2														
	3														
	4														
	5														
	6														
	7														
W E E K 2	8														
	9														
	10														
	11														
	12														
	13														
	14														
W E E K 3	15														
	16														
	17														
	18														
	19														
	20														
	21														
W E E K 4	22														
	23														
	24														
	25														
	26														
	27														
	28														
	29														
	30														
	31														
	T*														
	B*														
	D*														

* T = Total; B = Budget; D = Difference

		JAN.	FEB.	MAR.	APR.	MAY	JUNE	JULY	AUG.	SEPT.	OCT.	NOV.	DEC.	Total	Mo. Avg.
Net Income	Salary/Commission														
	Other														
Food	Groceries														
	School Lunches, Dine Out, Fast Food														
	Snacks, Beverages, Alcohol, Tobacco														
Household	Supplies, Cleaners, Maintenance, House, Yard, Pool														
	Appliances, Furniture, Furnishings, Supplies														
	Postage, ATM Fees, Bank Charges, Misc.														
	Interest, Taxes														
Transportation	Gas														
	Automobile Maintenance, Wash, License														
	Transit, Tolls, Taxi, Parking														
Personal	Clothing, Alterations, Dry Cleaning, Laundry, Shoe Care														
	Cosmetics, Hair, Nails, Massage, Toiletries														
Health	Doctor, Dentist, Vision, Medicine, Vitamins														
	Personal Growth Therapy														
Recreation	Vacation, Trips														
	Entertain., DVD, Movies, Music, Parties														
	Sports, Hobbies, Lessons, Clubs, Lottery														
	Computer, Upgrades, Software, Supplies, Service														

SUMMARY FOR MONTHLY SAVINGS/INVESTMENTS/RETIREMENT

	JAN.	FEB.	MAR.	APR.	MAY	JUNE	JULY	AUG.	SEPT.	OCT.	NOV.	DEC.	Total
Savings													
Investments													
Retirement													
Total													

END-OF-THE-YEAR TAX INFORMATION

		JAN.	FEB.	MAR.	APR.	MAY	JUNE	JULY	AUG.	SEPT.	OCT.	NOV.	DEC.	Total	Mo. Avg.
Education	Tuition, Supplies, Workshops, Seminars														
	Books, Magazines, Software, Newspaper, Games														
Family	Elder Care, Child Care, Sitter, Tutor														
	Allowance, Toys, Infant Exp., School Exp., Arcades														
	Pet, Vet, Supplies, Services														
General	Gifts, Cards, Flowers														
	Charitable Contribut., Church, Temple														
	Work Expense, Dues														
	Prof. Serv., Legal, CPA, Investment														
	Other														
Home	Mortgage, Rent, Assn. Fees														
Utilities	Gas, Electric														
	Water, Garbage														
	Phone, Cable, ISP														
Support	Child, Spousal, Club														
Insur.	Home, Auto, Life, Health, Disability, Storage														
Install.	Loans, Credit Cards														
Total	Monthly Expenses														

	JAN.	FEB.	MAR.	APR.	MAY	JUNE	JULY	AUG.	SEPT.	OCT.	NOV.	DEC.	Total
Federal													
State													
FICA													
Other Deductions													
Total													

MEDICAL EXPENSE RECORD

DOCTOR, DENTIST, AND HOSPITAL VISITS

Date	Mileage	To Whom Paid	Amount	Date Submitted	Insurance Reimbursements Amount/Date Paid
		Total			
		Total Amount Paid			
		Total Reimbursed			
		Total Medical Cost			

MEDICAL EXPENSE RECORD

MEDICAL EXPENSES, PRESCRIPTIONS, AND OTHER

Date	Mileage	To Whom Paid	Amount	Date Submitted	Insurance Reimbursements Amount/Date Paid
		Total			
		Total Amount Paid			
		Total Reimbursed			
		Total Medical Cost			

TAX-DEDUCTIBLE EXPENSE RECORD

Date	Description (Donation/Paym	Ch	Amount /Value:	Charitable		
			Total			

INVESTMENT/SAVINGS RECORD

RESERVE FUNDS (Checking, Savings, Money Market, etc.)

Name of Institution	Type	Account Number	Dat	Amo	Int	Owned By (husban

RETIREMENT ACCOUNTS (IRA, Roth, 401(k), 403(b), SEP, Keogh, etc.)

Where Held	Type and Name	Account Number	Purc	Am	Allocation

SHORT- AND LONG-TERM HOLDINGS (Mutual Funds, Stocks, Bonds, etc.)

Where Held	Type and Name	Certificate / Account	Purc	Am	Num	Unit	Dividend

OTHER (Real Estate, Collectibles, etc.)

Location/Name	Date	Cost	Monthly/Yearly	Location of Records

SAVINGS ACTIVITY RECORD

EMERGENCY

Institution: _____ Account Number: _____

	JAN	FEB	MAR	APR	MAY	JUN	JUL	AUG	SEPT	OCT	NOV	DEC
Deposits												
Withdraw												
Interest												
Balance												

RESERVE

Institution: _____ Account Number: _____

	JAN	FEB	MAR	APR	MAY	JUN	JUL	AUG	SEPT	OCT	NOV	DEC
Deposits												
Withdraw												
Interest												
Balance												

GOALS/CHRISTMAS AND HOLIDAY

Institution: _____ Account Number: _____

	JAN	FEB	MAR	APR	MAY	JUN	JUL	AUG	SEPT	OCT	NOV	DEC
Deposits												
Withdraw												
Interest												
Balance												

OTHER

Institution: _____ Account Number: _____

	J	F	MA	A	M	J	J	AUG	SEPT	OCT	NOV	DEC
Deposits												
Withdrawals												
Interest												
Balance												